TEXAS
RANGERS
STARS, STATS, HISTORY, AND MORE!
BY CONOR BUCKLEY

The Child's World®
childsworld.com

Published by The Child's World®
1980 Lookout Drive • Mankato, MN 56003-1705
800-599-READ • www.childsworld.com

ISBN 9781503828414
LCCN 2018944856

Printed in the United States of America
PAO2392

Photo Credits:
Cover: Joe Robbins (2).
Interior: AP Images: Al Messerschmidt 8; Newscom:
Steve Nuremberg/Icon SW 11, Roger Mallison/MCT 17,
Darrell Byers/KRT 19, Ken Murray/Icon SW DEL 20, An-
drew Dieb/Icon SW 27, Ron J. Jenkins 29; Joe Robbins: 4,
7, 12, 14, 23, 24.

About the Author

Conor Buckley is a lifelong
baseball fan now studying
for a career in esports. His
books in this series are his first
published works.

On the Cover

Main photo: Shortstop Elvis Andrus
Inset: former star catcher
Ivan Rodriguez

CONTENTS

GO, RANGERS!

The Texas Rangers have become one of the hottest teams in baseball. They have made it to two **World Series** in the past **decade**. They earned other playoff spots, too. Texas fans have not seen a World Series champion yet. They are still cheering, though! Let's meet the Texas Rangers!

◄ Third baseman Adrian Beltre is one of the best players in Rangers history.

WHO ARE THE RANGERS?

The Rangers play in the American League (AL). That group is part of Major League Baseball (MLB). MLB also includes the National League (NL). There are 30 teams in MLB. The winner of the AL plays the winner of the NL in the World Series.

Elvis Andrus shows off his speed on the basepaths. ➤

WHERE THEY CAME FROM

The Rangers used to play in Washington, DC. They were called the Senators. The Senators began play in 1961. For the 1972 season, the Senators moved. The team's new home was in Arlington, Texas, near Dallas. They took the name Texas Rangers. That's also the name of a famous group of state police officers.

◄ *Hall of Fame hitter Ted Williams was the manager of the Senators and Rangers from 1969 to 1972.*

WHO THEY PLAY

The Rangers play 162 games in a season. That's a lot of baseball! They play most of their games against other AL teams. The Rangers are part of the AL West Division. The other AL West teams are the Houston Astros, the Los Angeles Angels, the Oakland Athletics, and the Seattle Mariners. Texas also plays NL teams.

After a big win in 2018, the Rangers celebrated with a splash! ➤

WHERE THEY PLAY

he Rangers play in Globe Life Park in Arlington, Texas. It opened in 1994. Some of its parts were modeled after old-time ballparks like Yankee Stadium. The Rangers are moving to a new ballpark in 2020. It will have a roof that can close to protect fans from the heat of summer in Texas!

◄ *Check out the longhorn cattle that decorate the outside of the Rangers ballpark.*

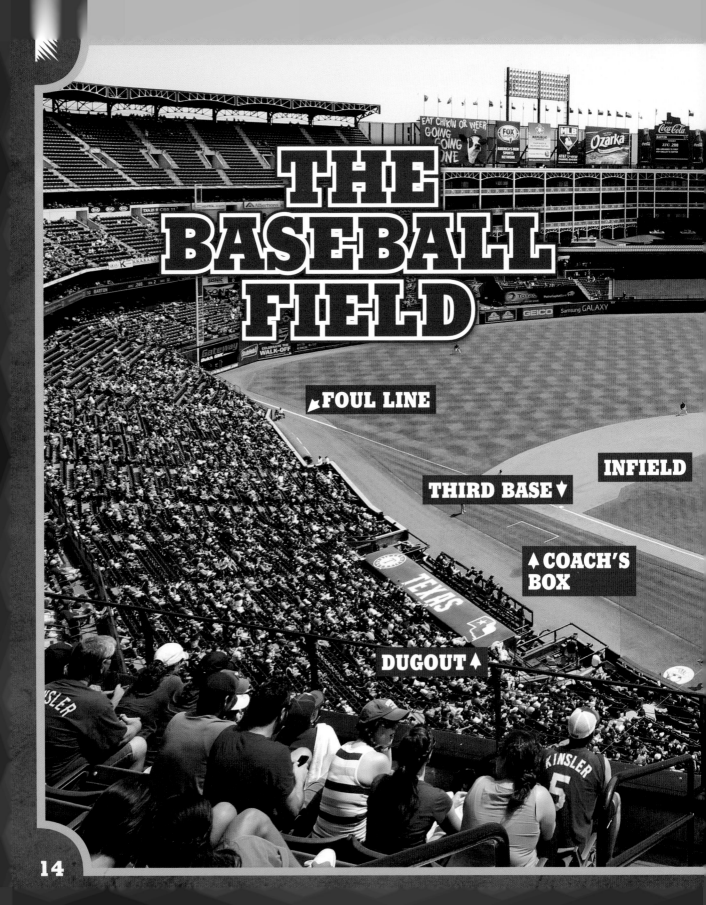

THE BASEBALL FIELD

FOUL LINE

INFIELD

THIRD BASE

COACH'S BOX

DUGOUT

OUTFIELD

◄ **SECOND BASE**

FOUL LINE ►

FIRST BASE ►

▲ **PITCHER'S MOUND**

▲ **HOME PLATE**

◄ **ON-DECK CIRCLE**

BIG DAYS

The Rangers are one of the newest teams in the AL. Here are some of their best performances.

1996—Texas won its first full-season AL West title. The Rangers lost in the playoffs, but it was a big step forward.

2007—The Rangers scored 30 runs while allowing only three to the Baltimore Orioles! The Rangers' runs were an all-time, single-game MLB best.

2010—The Rangers won their first AL championship. They made it to the World Series

Mitch Moreland high-fived with fans after ➤
Texas won the 2010 AL title.

TOUGH DAYS

Here's a look back at some games and seasons Rangers fans might want to forget!

1963—The Senators only had one winning record in 11 seasons in Washington. This year, the team set a record with 106 losses.

1993—Outfielder Jose Canseco hit a lot of homers for the Rangers. In a 1993 game, however, he made history. A ball hit by an **opponent** bounced off of Canseco's head. The ball went over the fence for a weird home run!

Oops! Michael Young couldn't handle this grounder. ➤
That's how it went in the Rangers' tough 2001 season.

2001—In Texas, this might have been the worst season. The Rangers finished 43 games out of first place!

MEET THE FANS!

Rangers fans love to see their team win. They don't even mind how hot it gets in the ballpark! Rangers Captain is the team **mascot**. It helps fans cheer for the Rangers. Rangers Captain is a giant horse. It wears the number 72. That stands for 1972, the team's first year in Texas.

◄ *Yee-ha! Rangers Captain gets a ride as he enters the field before a ballgame.*

HEROES THEN

Slugging outfielder Juan Gonzalez hit more homers than any other Rangers player. Infielder Michael Young played the most games for Texas. He also had the most hits. Young played shortstop and first base. Catcher Ivan Rodriguez played his first 12 seasons with the Rangers. He was a 10-time All-Star and the 1999 AL **Most Valuable Player**.

Ivan Rodriguez was a great defensive catcher and a solid hitter. ➤

HEROES NOW

Rougned Odor is a great all-around player. He hits homers and steals bases. Adrian Beltre is one of the top third basemen of all time. He has more than 3,000 hits in his career. Shin-Soo Choo is the **designated hitter**. He often leads the team in hits. Joey Gallo is the Rangers' top power hitter.

◄ *Shin-Soo Choo is one of only a few MLB players who are from Korea.*

GEARING UP

aseball players wear team uniforms. On defense, they wear leather gloves to catch the ball. As batters, they wear hard helmets. This protects them from pitches. Batters hit the ball with long wood bats. Each player chooses his own size of bat. Catchers have the toughest job. They wear a lot of protection.

THE BASEBALL

The outside of the Major League baseball is made from cow leather. Two leather pieces shaped like 8s are stitched together. There are 108 stitches of red thread. These stitches help players grip the ball. Inside, the ball has a small center of cork and rubber. Hundreds of feet of yarn are tightly wound around this center.

CATCHER'S MASK
AND HELMET

CHEST
PROTECTOR

WRIST
BANDS

CATCHER'S
MITT

SHIN GUARDS

CATCHER'S GEAR

TEAM STATS

ere are some of the all-time career records for the Texas Rangers. All these stats are through the 2018 regular season.

STOLEN BASES	
Elvis Andrus	270
Ian Kinsler	172

RBI	
Juan Gonzalez	1,180
Rafael Palmeiro	1,039

BATTING AVERAGE	
Al Oliver	.319
Will Clark	.308

STRIKEOUTS	
Charlie Hough	1,452
Bobby Witt	1,405

WINS	
Charlie Hough	139
Kenny Rogers	133

SAVES	
John Wetteland	150
Jeff Russell	134

Juan Gonzalez was a star for the Rangers from 1989 to 1999. ➤

HOME RUNS

| Juan Gonzalez | 372 |
| Rafael Palmeiro | 321 |

GLOSSARY

decade (DECK-ayd) a period of 10 years

designated hitter (DEZ-ig-nay-ted HIT-ter) known as the DH, this player bats in place of the pitcher in the American League

mascot (MASS-cot) a costumed character that helps fans cheer

Most Valuable Player (MOHST VALL-you-bull PLAY-er) an award given to the top player in each league

opponent (uh-PONE-ent) a team or a player who plays against your team

World Series (WURLD SEE-reez) the annual championship of Major League Baseball

FIND OUT MORE

IN THE LIBRARY

Connery-Boyd, Peg. *Texas Rangers: The Big Book of Baseball Activities*. Chicago, IL: Sourcebooks Jabberwocky, 2016.

Kelley, David A. *The Rangers Rustlers: Ballpark Mysteries No. 12*. New York, NY: Random House Books for Young Readers, 2016.

Sports Illustrated Kids (editors). *The Big Book of Who: Baseball*. New York, NY: Sports Illustrated Kids, 2017.

ON THE WEB

Visit our website for links about the Texas Rangers:
childsworld.com/links

Note to Parents, Teachers, and Librarians: We routinely verify our Web links to make sure they are safe and active sites. So encourage your readers to check them out!

INDEX